TIME SLIP

Time Slip

Terra Vagus

Contents

For who I have been and who I've always wanted to be.

And for The Sandman...thanks for the inspiration.

1

Breathe

Tea Towel

I am a tea towel
With a very specific purpose.

When I've found it
I know I'll be wonderful.

Until then I am mediocre.

The Gift of Presence

My anxieties are always chasing the future.

Frustration grows as I know
I will never leave the present.

I'll seclude myself from you
to include myself with me.

Nothing exists when I am alone.

I stop time.
Contemplate existence.

Nothing exists when I am alone.

But my skin still falls ever so slightly with each thought
passing me by.

A cruel reminder that I am wrong.

Even when my clock stops.
The world clock tick-tocks.

As I relentlessly obsess over what comes next
I abandon the present.

I abandon the future.

I am stuck in a construct of my own lifeline.

I'm unsure how to see outside this frame of mind.

My ego is my enemy.
My only security.

The present comes packaged with a ribbon
that I don't have the guts to undo.

Interruptions

Cannon fire is something I've never heard authentically.
Much like many words of comfort I seem to have

Missed out along my way. Who would I be
if not for the wrongdoings I've experienced?
Possibly I'd be brave enough

To fall asleep with the lights off
long before I creep out of my twenties.
The monsters in the closet,

they were real.
I've stitched my fearful pieces back together
with what little hope I've got. After each piece of darkness
spat me back into the light.

Slightly weaker.

Even the light is lonely.
Monsters find their way discreetly.
They see my misery. Though they pay no mind.
What's happened to me is an inconvenience

of the worst kind. For what's happened to me,
I keep finding, I apologize. Like cannons on the television,
I bellow regrets each time I open my mouth
to spill this darkness out.

Keep quiet so as to not dim other's light.
Simply never find yourself back in the dark,
you may just die of fright.

Working Class

Arguably,
The world is bleak.
Although I'm told
I've got it at my feet.

What I see is concrete.

My watering can sits empty.
All poured out hopelessly.
Trying to sprout a garden that this ground
just won't set free.

My shovel gains flattened edges,
As I try to break through an obstacle made by man
To block the world from those like me.

Aged hands.
Aged face.
An aged human,

Forced in one place.

Countless others working just the same.
To plant any seed.
We'll give all but our name.
Before the concrete finally crumbles.

All we want is a sprout from our seeds.

Memento Vivere

Constant daydreams of the life I long to lead
Interrupted by reality
tossing a lasso 'round my ankle.

Pulling down-
my head from the clouds.
In an emergency kit,
I've got the plans.

Not the guts.
I have been forever consumed searching for them.
Daily interactions fail to lead others
Beyond the parlor of my mind.

I wait in my crimson chair-
Eyes fixed, hardly present.
Watching the time.

Waiting to make my retreat.

To plot and to plan
the transformation of what it is that I am.
I don't believe I belong in this parlor
I've done up just for you.

One day I'll cut your lasso.
I'll pull my sky on top of me.

Maybe I'm Self Sabotaging. Maybe It's Genetic.

I feel as though my eyes deceive me. I spy cracks
running through the concrete.
Run gives way to sprint.
The concrete penetrates my life.
My foundation. Sturdy.
Was only meant to be temporary.
I fill each sprinting crack with trinkets I consume.
Needlessly.
Not concrete. They crumble.
I crumble.

Destined to break away
in dusty fragments. What remains
will be fade-outs of your voice.
I told you so.
You told me so.

Permanence scares me. One false move
and even wet concrete holds you down.
Holds *me* down. Till I'm grey and perhaps wiser.
Wiser yet still unable to move. Held in place, not by fear
but slowly sinking further and further
as I'm swallowed by regret.

Only when I'm long gone will this concrete
completely crack.
Crumble away.

Desperately I try to fill the void
with anything opposite of fear.
Buy this. Collect that.
Place them in the cracks. Do they fit?

Am I happy now?

The Eyes I Feel Watching Me Are My Own

Who is driving my car
as I'm off in my nightmare from last night?
Scenes crowded with creatures. Faceless.
Growing closer in the flickering light.
Humming.
Hissing sounds of static. Leaving me frantic.

My curiosity pales in comparison to my fears.
Possibly they have a message. No Use.
It won't get through. They scream now.
This white noise grows louder.
I can't take it. I clasp my ears.

The hairs on my neck rise-
the way they do when you're watched
by demon eyes. I've realized this nightmare-
it's my life. The thought crosses
once more. Who is driving my car?

These creatures. This demon. Don't know harm
from good. My eyes play tricks
throughout the day. When I glance
into the mirror, not a demon
in my backseat. Worse.
Tears make their way out. I cannot look away.
In my backseat. Always watching. Not a demon.
I see me. Who is driving my car?

The Saddest Songs Are Silent

A gust of wind has carried away the last note of song

in my life. I can only imagine how silent it would be
if not for the chaos inside.

I exist. I exist. Oh my God. I think I'd prefer an abyss
to waiting in terror for an end to this.

Each apple I eat is sour. Each tune I've heard is off-key.
Each man I've met is guilty. Each woman I've met is me.

Set me free. Set me free.

Not to death but to understanding.

I exist.
I exist.

A crisis of a thought.
Upon no one would I wish it. Sing your tune louder,
stand taller, prouder. It's dark when you realize

you are small. Meaningless
in a seemingly never-ending well.
Dug by what?

My crisis.

Jack

I walked into a room
to see a man
putting back shots of holy water.

He asked if I could help him
get out of his mind.

There was a party inside,
and he wasn't invited.

To watch a person rot from the inside out
is such a disastrous sight.

My eyes stay fixed.

I watched a man attempt to drown his demons.
I watched a man attempt to stop the screaming.

My eyes stay fixed.

What terrors must exist in the human mind
to make a man turn whiskey into holy water
just to feel the privilege

of sitting in silence?

My eyes stay fixed.

Vita

A stalemate.
Game of chess.

Can't shake selfishness.
Though I feel I desire more.
A barren waste,
cold to its core.

Not one shred of life.
Not one seed will grow.

A harsh tundra,
dark as night,
sees to it
that all is lost.

Upon my shoulders,
an angel tells me to flip on the light.
Welcome life.
A demon says the same.
Yet, they hesitate.

A fear of scrutiny lingers.

Lack of faith in my own abilities,
my own tenderness.

I swallow another pill.

Chills

At the sky, I stare.
You see I'm yelling at thin air.
I see the shape of all my despair.
A life I can't recall follows me each day.
Yells at me that I'm getting in the way.
I'm sick.
I'm sick.
How did I get like this?
I can't remember.
Can't even remember if I want to get better.
Sleeping outside seems fine
when you can't imagine anything else.
Take my youth.
Put it on a shelf.
Bet Momma never knew this world would give us Hell.
She doesn't call anymore.
When I come around she knows what's in store.
I don't wanna live like this.
But somehow I want more.
Judge me harshly as you do.
We're both ill. Me differently than you.

Birthday Party

Your slow decay gives reason to celebrate.
So eat your cake and await your fate.
She's the one guest who's never late.

Letters from the Monster

This is not a resurrection. I am only half a human
with all but half a life. A rotting shell frightened of myself.
No one cares to wonder what it is
that makes the monster afraid.

Who wants to believe
their nightmares might be human? When comfort
is pretending they aren't there.

A poisoned diet
consumed from youth brews a time bomb bubbling.
Identity vanished
behind a mask
to blend with radical norms.
Watch the bomb erupt in flames.
The last ingredient-
a dash of rage.
What once was a shell
of a mere human in Hell
is now a zombie escaped from the grave.

Believe that monsters can too feel terror
as they're merely reflections of human error.
Monsters are only as frightening
as the human truth.
The truth about your movies?
The monster lives in you.

Self Reflections

At times I am brave enough
To gaze upon my reflection
A little bit longer.

A possible attempt to see me
From the sight of another.

Yet, there's no hard line
Between what I imagine
And what is true.

I am no longer brave.

Left with wounded feelings from this view.

Loose Leaf

My kettle brews with images of heaven
made up in its steam.

As I move to pour
my teacup cracks.

Weary of the heat.

The same warmth which moves my kettle to song
causes my cup to shriek.

The cup now ages in a cupboard.
No tea is served today.

Dimensions

I've seen myself as a ghost
wandering through corridors and doorways.
I've felt envy toward this reflection of me
who walks so freely into rooms
I could hardly dream.

I remain trapped in this hallway
stunned by fear.
These doors aren't locked up.
I am.

Funny how this ghost of me exists quite freely.
Unsettling is that she seems the same age as me.

In the mirror I see her
paying me no mind.
We've never looked at each other.
Never seen eye to eye,
She's everything I wish I could be.

I'm forever haunted by this better version of me.

Snow on Charade

My expectations have never been low.
As a child, I would look at salt
and I would call it snow.

Not sugar, but something a little more sweet.

Magic from the sky that would bury my feet.

Anticipation grew as I prepared to taste.
Only to spit it out and let it waste.

Not one drop of magic.

I blamed the snow for this charade.

From that moment forth, I hated winter days.

Not once did I pause.
Pause and think
maybe, just maybe
there was no charade.
Not salt nor snow can take the blame.

I should have realized then
each one is unique
and these false expectations
came from me.

Maps

They can look past my bruises
but these are what made me.

I was grown from different landscapes and phases.
My mind is nothing but thousands of places.

An Option Not To Drown

Air fills each lung at last.
Last time I'll fall into the sea.
Sea of dark, cold, overwhelming pressure.
Pressure to do better than before.
Before I even realized expectations could be so high.
High on anything to numb the pain.
Pain from the monster draining my life.
Life fading out until I see the light.
Light from both directions, both leading to an end.
End of all my days, or end of just one part.
Part of me that needs to die so I can once more grow.
Grow the strength to swim above the pressures of the sea.

See the moonlight cheer me on
as I once more start to breathe.

Gypsum Rose

A Gypsum Rose is thrown from a desert storm.
Thrown from the rain into a dust parade.
Hold this Gypsum Rose and all its harsh petals.
Still continue to clutch it tight
as the storm falls to the floor.

Who are these people with only half faces?
In these times, forever condemned as strangers
in unfamiliar places.

Inhale dirt. Exhale peace.
I sweep the storm in attempt to tidy.
I see hard work and hungry eyes but still,
the rest is hiding.

Caught in a hurricane without the rain
in a world which I adore.
When warmth swaddles me, this chaos subsides.
I am invited to see. To stand within its eye.

In my pocket sits my Gypsum Rose which does not bloom.
Among the friction of my clothing, it remains
graciously resilient.
I grasp it tightly in my hand and with it
I begin to understand
why my Gypsum Rose does not bloom.

Its environment is harsh yet not unkind.

Requires adaptation to weather each storm.
A Gypsum Rose does not bloom,
but like the desert sun, it shines.

2

Bleed

Pavement

I always imagined
that when I fell in love
my heart would glow.

Not like the glow of a firework
demanding attention.

But the glow of wet pavement
at midnight
underneath the streetlights.

Beckoning

comforting

Glow.

Buried in the Walls

If you could briefly breathe into me
the light that shines for you.

I'd like to borrow it
only for a moment,
to adjust my point of view.

I can't see past these eyelids
closing curtains on my world.
Been fumbling in the dark
with my eyes sealed shut by terror.

I don't dare open
or let you gaze within.
I worry of your judgment
when you peer into my sin.

Seeping through the wall I've built
is your persistence to be close.
I block you out yet miss you so-
have a permanent lump in my throat.

Can't let you see each part of me
I'm so scared you'll leave.

I can hear you
banging on the wall
trying to set me free.

Cautious Reverence

Most people I admire
I do so from a distance.

I don't want to risk ruining
the qualities I believe to be true.

Silentium

I was taught to bite my tongue
before I knew to crawl.

Silenced in such a way,
those I spent the most time with
hardly knew my sound.

listen.
listen.

If they would like to know a thing about you,
they will surely ask.

I kept my world in a bottle.
You handed me the cork.

Over time all I've known is pressure from within
as it overflows with all I've kept inside.

Still, I try.

As a voice echoes toward me
Listen. Don't share.
I've long been groomed to believe not a soul could care.

Even as I age,
in conversation I am disciplined.

I am hushed.

My teeth are the guillotine
that cuts off what I feel in my own heart.

As you speak, I hold my breath.
I hear a hum from my bottle.

Violent.

On the verge of shattering.
Layers of sad tape pretend to seal old cracks.
I exhale only when I'm alone.

For you,
I am poised.

As I am an ear for your story,
I am for a lifetime unable to share mine.

Perfect Lie

A perfectionist
in an imperfect state of mind.
Often self-comforting,
making up lullabies.
How I've always gone about
not being good enough.

I am a flower,
only caught in a drought.

Love me.
Water me.

Silent pleads for release each fall flat
when out loud I reassure that I am capable.

I'm not.

Believe in me.
But don't let me be.

Standing tall
in misery.

You walk away.
I soothe myself.

I am capable.

Fragrant

Their world smelled of
black coffee
and cigarette smoke.
Only just a little sweeter.
Almost smelled like
home.

Flower's Journey

Wilted flowers aren't given enough romance.

Tossed in the trash.

Lived beyond their bloom.
Or never bloomed at all.
Spent every hot month trying,
only to die in the fall.

Never considered beautiful.

A shriveled, slight window in a closed petal curtain
shows a glimpse of what vibrancy could have been.

Do we love flowers?

Or only when they bloom?

I imagine the flower's journey
and start to think of you.

I begin to appreciate growth from seed to bloom.
I now find romance in each flower I view.

Forest Fire

I'll have to run rather than stride
to avoid you burning me alive.

You don't realize what you're doing.
Each step and breath
you ignite this forest I've spent so long creating.

We once plucked all the flowers for their beauty
only to watch each one die faster than the last.

We should have grown more.
Or maybe
should have nurtured this forest floor
that I'm watching ignite.

You've engulfed every part of me
and have me confused on what's left.

Can I regrow these woods to sustain my life once more?

Or do I move along and plant anew?

Next time I find a lovely flower,
I'll be sure to appreciate the forest too.

Fire Blanket

Silence
in an instant.
Then we progress to sadness.
To madness.
To a calm still.
Before what lies beneath roars to the surface.

You never did express yourself well.
Always thinking I can read minds.
How could that possibly be? I can't even comprehend
what happens in my own.

I try to find a way without looking foolish
to make you pull me close.
The intimacy of closeness-
of touch amidst chaos
has become necessity.

I am one who has been taught from early stages
that to be open,
to be vulnerable,
is nothing more than an inconvenience to those near me.

At last, I've broken. No.
Something else.
I'm frightened.
Able to feel my body sink into this sea of gasoline.
The world strikes its match on the surface of humanity.

Before it hits this poison water
one more time,
touch my skin.
Hold me tight as if your sole purpose
is to keep my flesh on my bones
as everything else burns away.

Swimming Alone

Optimism is fleeting.
As is the sunlight.

I took a dip in the water to wash away the hurt.

All at once, the clouds rolled in.
I began to choke on the waves
as the world shifted into grey.

Are you a pessimist if you've learned from experience?

I know how to swim.
Though I'm being held down trying to keep others afloat.
I am far too empathetic.
They would let me drown.

How do I kick off and move on?
Give myself what I deserve?

I'm trying to shove off this deadweight
but my silly heart tells me
hang on.
If life is a quest for happiness
can I trust those that push me down?

If they hold me under I need to let them go.
It's awfully frightening swimming alone.

Red Sea

Someone drained me
of all that I have,
of all that I am.

The kindest knife
I've ever had.
Slowly pricking me
each and every day.

I will lift you when you fall.
Yet never notice-
each small wound you've carved into my hand
as you grasp it.

I wonder where this blood has come from.
You hand me a small bandage.
But I am the Red Sea.
Your patronizing help, is you seizing opportunity.

You manipulate my kindness.

You've made my anxiety your greatest weapon.

I am exhausted.
You've convinced me it's my own fault.
While you're the blade splitting my skin,
this blood runs only from me.

A narcissist in hand-
is only a knife in the heart.
Feeding me tales of how it's all my fault
for even loving you from the start.

Blinded by the Sun

I wanted to chase moonlight with you,
but the clouds wouldn't let it shine through.

Telling me you aren't the one.

I wanted to show you night skies,
but you were blinded by the sun.

Sunny Six Feet Under

All hail the end of me.
I'm succumbing to the misery.

Words I speak softly into my mirror.
I swear my reflection sneers.
Why couldn't the end be triumphant?
A parade.
An ovation.
Blasts of trumpets.

Celebrate me doing what I'm told
by my own internal monologue.
Leaving what I hate the most,
the cold.

Instead, I'm restrained by the guilt I feel
every time my imagination tunes to your sorrow.
You want me here. Tell me you need me.
Why does love make us so greedy?

I don't dare show my worst moments to you.
Oh god, you'd reject me.
Isn't it funny how both your love
and rejection frighten me to misery?

I'll just keep smiling. For you.
But please hand me one more blanket.
I can't stand the cold.

Tricks

I see malevolence in every corner of my life,
as my mind continues playing tricks on my eyes.

Every day is Halloween
when you believe everyone is in disguise.

I tried to force myself to trust.
It's not so bad.

TREASON.
BETRAYAL.

I've placed a knife in my own back
by offering to hold it for you.
Now I cannot retrieve it.
I can see what you're really saying,

Leave it.

For years I have.
We've become mostly united.
Only a twinge on occasion,
to make me think of you.

I see your shadow now in every place.
Inside the eyes of even the most innocent face.

You've gifted me fear.

Thank you.
I hate it.

Now I'm cursed with this daily plight,
attempting to reteach my mind
that it isn't always right.

Not every soul shrouds a monster inside.
Not every soul is you.

Chocolate

I count the moments that pass as a piece of chocolate
melts in my mouth.
Each is a moment I don't need to make an excuse
for my silence.
I'm not prepared for the repercussions
of my own thoughts.
So I consume them with every drip of chocolate
that slides down my throat.

In my stomach, these thoughts eat me alive.
Wish it were butterflies
but these are vicious wasps and agony.

Growth is uncomfortable.
Moving on feels like madness.
Emotional scars run the deepest.
All my dizziest daydreams are consumed by negativity.

I feel sick.
Or I am sick.
There's no way to tell anymore.

When my mouth frees up I'd like to sew it shut.
I don't think I could help myself from spilling my guts
while you believe
I'm moving on.

'Til Death

If you were a ghost would you come back to me?
Or would you leave this world and be set free?
Would you haunt me until my days are few?
If I were a ghost, I'd stay with you.
Yes, if I were a ghost I think I'd wait forever.
Until the day comes we'll be ghosts together.

Empty Words

Day in and day out
the constant coos of *I love yous*
have almost lost their meaning.

Just a phrase as natural as *hello.*
Until it's lost its meaning

Words echo louder when they're empty.

Red Flags Stained With Blood

I got a lot I can't seem to write down. How it feels to know
I need to be done with you.

To break my own heart. Making excuses to stay silent
and pretend you're a better person than you are.

You've made me into one big scar.
You believe that's just my skin.
Think I'm naïve.

You could capture every tear I've cried
and still find a way to blame it all on me.
You never truly left

but abandoned me just the same. Now it's time
to draw a line in this coarse sand
to keep my past and my future at a distance.

Because my present is screaming.
My heart hasn't before broke like this.
I hope I do better. I hope you learn one day

why I've decided to cut
what thin thread held us together in the first place.
I can't bear to think of who you really are. I need to leave
while I'm still able to conjure up a mental image

of the you I've always wanted to believe in.
While I'm still able to love you.
While it still hurts. Heartbreak means love.
Or maybe that's what a person thinks

when they're alone in their car
looking back on moments of their life
that could have exposed everything
right before their eyes.

If only I were wiser.
Or heartless.
Or anything other than this.

Painted Dead

Mistakes were made with myself.
Patience is a virtue I've never possessed.

So I wash myself in red.

Too preoccupied with presentation
to care who saw through.

Trapped in a room.
Never learned
how to bloom.

I am a hallucination.
Master of adaptation.
A garden for whatever it is others seek.

Unwanted when not a necessity.

Painted myself red.
My least favorite color.
If only to grant myself allure.

You asked-
I have been.
Avoiding you.
To tend to me.

For the world, I disguised myself in red.
Turns out the roses I hid behind were dead.

In the dark, I wait
for the water to wash the red from me.

Planted.

Patiently.

Petals and Ash (*I would die for you*)

Blessed with a curse
the red flower is
exquisitely erect.

Delicate sways in the wind.
Though she broods over life.

A future of war.

Pain striking at all angles.
Stretching, contorting, ripping.
Until a thief of identity arrives bearing the coldest snow.

The red flower loves them so.

Buried in snow 'til she can no longer stand.
One gust of wind and her petals dance.
All the way
to the ground.

Until all that remains is a pile of death.
Petals and ash are all that is left.

The last smoke rises.
A gift for the thief.
Last love.
Last embrace.
Last petal floats off in the breeze.

3

Bury

Soft Water

Would almost rather float with apathy
than continue drowning in my empathy.

My inner currents never reflect my outer actions.
I didn't mean to live so amiably.

I've watched countless opportunities
be snatched up in nets

by those whose feelings
I was always so concerned for.

If I could go back in time
tell my child self

They don't care like you do.

I think I'd be stronger.
No longer a pond without threat,
but the great sea I know myself to be.

My water reflects much too softly for this world.

Burn Out

The candle is struck.
I watch the wick
appear and vanish.
A wax overcoat slides
onto the dessert underneath. I can only be
transfixed on what is happening to me.

Struck to burn I was.
What seems so long ago.

Though I know I've aged,
I can't help but feel callow.
Running out of time to design my ending.

Not of old age yet, but able to feel my skin tailor and adjust
to what I am becoming.
My own wax dripping down.
What a pleasing sight I am.

Until I burn out.

Apathy

Curiosity kills the heart.

Apathy rots the soul.

How does one find peace
before this world can eat them whole?

Muddy Boots

The lake turned into a pond.
The pond turned into a puddle.
The puddle turned into mud.
When I glanced down at my muddy boots

I realized my days are numbered.

Good Things

Save yourself
from negativity.
If they bring you down-
set them free.

Lost friends can hurt our hearts too.
But there's so many other pieces of you.

Love yourself.
Your heart will mend.
Some good things-
are just meant to end.

Dead Ends

A drink with friends

to our dead ends

may as well be dying alone.

Parting Gift

I grew tired of being controlled.
So I did the only thing I knew.

I plucked my rib like a flower.
Handed it to you.

A parting gift.

Ghosts

I couldn't cope with the past.
I couldn't live in the present.
I sacrificed my future.

I wanted silence.
But the whispers sound like screams.

I am in darkness.
But I am not alone.
I can hear the ghosts surrounding me.

The past is laughing, for they have won.
The present is angry, for they were ignored.
The future gently weeps.

Exhale

Heart weakly drumming.
Body fatigued from its fight.
Brain passed in battle.
It couldn't bear another thought.
Rapid beeping tones turn to a most lengthy somber tune.

One last exhale none can see.

War has ended.
You are free.

Brightest Light

The brightest light
we'll ever see must be
our life replaying
right before
we say goodbye.

Crossroads

My bones broke in my feeble efforts
to outlast the longest life.
Turned to dust behind the skin that's hanging on
with all its might.

All my food is liquid
and my family already cries.
I pushed so far, for I was scared of my own time to die.

Reapers surround each of my sides.
Assure me I won't feel hurt.
I'm lifted gently
and moved slow.
Wasn't long till they had me on the road.

My bones no longer felt so fragile.
My skin felt wonderfully new.

Cloaked in black.
Here to guide me.
A promise to help me through.

No longer left with fear of the end.
These reapers carried me and we talked like old friends.
I laughed and reminisced on my life.
Of all my years among the living
this has been my most pleasant ride.

Insect

The insect told me

We have always been equals.

Then continued to eat my body.

Seven Feet Deep

I opened wide the gates of Hell
to explore your world at its core.
I am not cowardly.
Still, I am frightened just the same.
Moments last ages as I cross over.
Imprisoned in an unfamiliar place.

I never did dance with the Devil.
Though more than once I've found myself
a wallflower present at his affairs.

I am the observer.
Not from Heaven.
Not from Hell.
Sent to watch.
Never to dwell.

I come and go as I please.
Showing immodest bravery
as I shut your doors behind me.
Turning my back to you. Unafraid.

I am a living, breathing middle ground.
Not to be condemned nor saved.
They'll curse my grave when the time comes.
Even in death, if you can't fit the proper box,
you are an enemy.
They'll bury me down one foot deeper than the rest.

Place weight on my chest.

My home is to roam and I roam where my soul is called.
I am no longer called to you. More so I am tired of waiting
for this Devil Man to take my hand.
So I have saved myself.

Always off to where my soul is called.
To strip this heaviness away.
To drink the venom of which you fear, let it glow
and guide out my true self.
Not quite fearless. Yet all the more brave.
Behind me, I lock your gates to Hell.

Fog

No one ever warned me when the storm of grief subsides,
I'd still spend so many days lost in the fog.

Sneaker Waves

Learning not to be angry
with those who robbed me.

Put their ego above all others.

I never got the traditional opportunity
to experience your loss.

Now I learn to be with my grief.

A constant flow of tides
with an occasional sneaker wave.

If I'm not cautious
an entire ocean will swallow me whole.

Freezing waves of anger and sorrow
slamming against every inch of my weakened state.

I'm in no shape
to swim away.

I am only half a spirit anymore.

Until my other half learns
to stop searching for you.

Webs and Headstones

I bathe with the lights off
when no one is home.

To draw no attention
as I let my past rot.

Through a window, I see a spider has made a home.
An intricate web
with raindrops to light every angle.

Perhaps they're tears of mourning
from Earth herself
for the lives lost within the web's beauty.

My past is a life lost
for which I cannot mourn.

There's no headstone in the realm
which my old self ends up
as I let it twirl down the drain.

Each new self

each new web

brings growth in spite of pain.

One More Lifetime

I can't recall a single night you haven't crossed my mind.
Driving me mad
each time I reach out, unable to grasp your hand.

Figment of my grief.
Haunter of my dreams.

You've left me with far too little memories.
I'm only asking for one more lifetime with you.

Andy

Black coffee smells like-

early mornings and memories
of when I was young and not allowed
to indulge in such things.

Tobacco smells like-

early mornings and conversations
I never counted on ending.

I never knew I'd miss you for such a length of time.

Never stepped outside myself
to realize our separate journeys
until my last hug to you that night on that gurney.

I really don't know that you even knew it was me.

Grieving your departure was a robbed opportunity.

Now I'm trapped with flash floods of sadness
and painful memories.

Forever longing for just one more morning of
black coffee, tobacco
and conversations with you.

November Air

At October's end, I'm left exhausted. A lifelong enemy.
October beats me till I'm blue. Drowns my mind
in emotional abuse.
The whole month is one long breeze.
Cold enough it snaps my bones. My eyes glaze over.
I retreat within. Waiting for October's end.

O October. She is bitter. My attempts at loving her
she spits back in a rage.
October. She taught me how to feel
the worst pains I've ever known.

Each fall my thoughts darken and sink
downward with the autumn leaves.
The rose-colored glasses I don for the summer
now paint October red.
Treelines so vibrant they break through each lens
to display a kaleidoscope of grief.

Thirty-One days I hold my breath and hide.
I lack the courage to face October's eyes.
Thirty-One days awaiting Samhain's end.
November air lends me the courage
to leave it all behind.

Burning Bridges

I've been burning sage
to cleanse life's negativity.

I've been burning bridges
that lead to places I don't need to be.

I've been loving old faces,
though only as memories.

I've been following life's instruction
on moving on from past destruction.

To Aaron. My Moon:

Thank you for your unwavering encouragement and support. Another thank you for your patience, collaborations, and willingness to drive across various terrains with me and a two-dollar thrift store sheet so that Terra Vagus may come to fruition.

You're truly the best there ever could be.

Photo by: Aaron Olvera

Terra Vagus is a lover of coffee, tea, and anything that has the scent or taste of rosemary. Writing is their first passion. The paranormal is their second.

At this point in their life, they've lived in six states and more cities than they can remember.

Home is a state of mind.